STRUCK DOWN BUT NOT DESTROYED

First published 2012 by Fast-Print Publishing of Peterborough, England.

www.fast-print.net/store.php

Struck Down But Not Destroyed

ISBN: 978-178035-346-3

A catalogue record for this book is available from the British Library

An environmentally friendly book printed and bound in England by www.printondemand-worldwide.com

This book is made entirely of chain-of-custody materials

This book is dedicated to my children,
Deborah and Christopher;
I love you both more than anyone
else on earth.

We stand or fall as a family;
we rise above our circumstances by
the grace of God.

"You will know the truth, and the
truth will set you free."
(John 8:32)

STRUCK DOWN BUT NOT DESTROYED

THE SPIRITUAL BIOGRAPHY OF CLIVE JACKSON

(as told to Diane Morrison)

"...persecuted but not forsaken; struck down but not destroyed; always carrying in the body the death of Jesus, so that the life of Jesus may be made visible..." *(2Corinthians 4:9-10 NRSV)*

One

War Baby

It is night. Along a dark road in East Dulwich a man is walking, his stride purposeful. A small boy trails behind him. This place is strange to the boy; the two of them have come what seems to be a very long way and he is tired and hungry, but there's nothing unusual in that – grubby as a street urchin, his bony limbs protrude from ill-fitting clothes, and his face is pinched and pale beneath his cap.

Despite the fact that the wartime blackout ended a year ago only a single streetlight glows, illuminating, as they pass beneath it, the bars of the dismantled cot the man carries under his arm. The boy's eyesight is marred by a squint, and he sees the cot as floating strangely in mid air, but nothing that has happened to him in the three years of his life has made much sense and very little of it has brought him any joy, so he walks on, head down, unquestioning and unexpectant.

Round the next corner, he is suddenly halted by a hand on the shoulder and a garden gate creaks as he is pushed through. Ahead, a door opens at once, as if those inside have been watching and listening, and the boy is ushered into the house and through a hallway, the sound of tense adult voices above his head.

In the kitchen, all he sees at first is a central table taller than he is, and then a man and a lady whose faces he knows smiling broadly at him – but what makes the biggest impression on him is the electric light, shining more brilliantly than any light he has ever known.

The light that says 'welcome home.'

*

The young, Welsh girl called Joyce Hughes was not the first to succumb to the wartime charms of a US serviceman; not the first to find herself pregnant, nor the first to believe his promises that he would come back and take both her and their baby to make a life with him in America. This man, though, had a better excuse than many for not returning – his ship hit a mine and, along with everyone else on board, he was killed. Clive was born in St Giles Hospital, Camberwell, on the fourth of June 1946, and soon afterwards Joyce was living with another man called Tim in Somerleyton Road, Peckham. It is this house that her son remembers as his first home.

Clive has an unusually acute and accurate recollection of his childhood – perhaps in compensation for the dyslexia that makes it difficult for him to record or read anything – but his recollections of this very early time are understandably few and hazy. It seems likely, however, that Joyce was already suffering from the same bipolar disorder that has dogged Clive throughout his life. Caused by a chemical imbalance in the brain, the condition runs in families, and can be triggered by traumatic events, such as the death of someone close, or by physical, emotional or sexual abuse. Joyce was subject to most, perhaps all of these. After the awful loss of the father of her son, she had made an unfortunate choice of replacement partner in Tim.

Clive's earliest memory is of crawling around in the back of the lorry that Tim drove. He also remembers his favourite toy – a squeaky barrel out of which the figure of a little man popped when it was squeezed – and trips to the park with Tim's Alsatian dog, Rex, of whom he was very fond. Mostly, though, his impressions of life at Somerleyton Road are dark and unpleasant. Joyce simply could not understand figures and money, and often made mistakes with prices and change. When this happened, Tim would beat her. She had very little idea of how to care for a child, no one to turn to for help and was in all probability suffering from depression, a common adjunct of bipolarism and similarly misunderstood in the forties. The young Clive was frequently left caged in his cot in soiled clothes for long periods and rarely had enough to eat.

Somewhere towards the end of his third year, something so awful happened that he has blanked it from his mind ever since. He knows he was in his cot and dirty, he knows it involved a man – presumably Tim. Whether it involved assault, abuse or both he cannot say, but for the story of the rest of his time in that house he has to rely on second-hand tales told to him by his adoptive mother: there is a black hole in his own memory.

While all this was going on, George and Margaret Jackson were living in nearby East Dulwich, happily married for ten years but unable to have children of their own – a matter of great unhappiness for them. Margaret first met Joyce walking in the park with Clive and Rex, and the two women got into the habit of sitting on a bench and talking together. From the first it was very obvious to Margaret that all was far from well. Clive was lethargic, appallingly skinny and evidently much neglected and her heart, full with frustrated motherhood, ached to do something about it. As she saw Joyce's own condition deteriorate, Margaret desperately wanted to rescue Clive and talked her husband into applying for an adoption.

Events were precipitated when something happened at Somerleyton Road that caused the authorities to intervene. Clive has never been able find out what – maybe it was the incident in his cot that his mind is still protecting him from – but whatever it was, a judge gave the Jacksons permission to take the three-year-old Clive into their family and "give him a Christian upbringing".

After his late-night delivery he never saw Joyce again and came to think of the Jacksons as his 'real' parents, but that first arrival at their home in Archdale Road, with just the clothes he was wearing and his cot, made an indelible impression on him. He had not experienced electric light before and its brilliance dazzled him; rarely had he seen such beaming smiles directed at him; and he had never owned anything so wonderful as the red wellington boots his new mother bought him the next day, and which he refused to take off, even in bed.

In a post-war world awash with orphans, and by the limited understanding of the time, everything had been done for him that was needful. He had been removed from the old, bad environment and placed in this new, good one, and was expected to thrive. Those first important three years were not to be shaken off so easily, however, and a plethora of new and unsuspected problems were soon to raise their ugly heads. The battle had only just begun. The darkness had not done with him yet.

*

The Jacksons were warm and generous people; natural parents whose ingenuity and bountiful supplies of patience were to be tested to the limits over the subsequent years. Firm, loving discipline came from Margaret, and was at first often resented by the little boy who had never known anything like it in his life. George, a night-shift print worker for the Daily Mail, he remembers as the 'soft' one. It was George who went to Battersea Dogs Home and brought back an Old English sheepdog called Bud to make up for the loss of Rex and to be a fellow adoptee for Clive. Boy and dog became inseparable and Bud was soon a well-known character in the neighbourhood, going to fetch the papers from the newsagent and sneaking rides in the back of police cars.

This was a time of constant new experiences for Clive – long walks, kicking up the leaves with his beloved red wellies, learning nursery rhymes like Humpty Dumpty and being read bedtime stories like

Jack and the Beanstalk – simple pleasures common to most childhoods but unknown to him. The Jacksons were part of a large and convivial extended family on both sides and, for the first time, Clive knew uncles, aunts and grandparents – he had a special affinity with Margaret's brother, Pat, a war hero, whom he idolised. During this time he had an operation to cure his squint and cauterisation to stop his constant nosebleeds. He lost his skeletal look and his Welsh accent and both his health and spirits improved.

But life was not all joy. The trauma of being confined to his cot back at Somerleyton Road and neither changed nor allowed to go to the toilet had left deep scars. He had a bed to sleep in now, but was terrified of the dark and had to have a nightlight, while the whole issue of using the toilet was traumatic and difficult for reasons neither he nor his new parents really understood. He still regularly wet and soiled the bed and would sometimes resist defecating for long periods of time.

One day Margaret took him and Bud to the park, then left him playing on the playground swings while she went to the dog-walking area. He had not 'gone' in days and was suddenly desperate to go and terrified, with two fences between him and his mother. Screaming in panic he managed to get over one fence and then clung to the second one crying and soiling himself while Margaret tried helplessly to comfort and quiet him from the other side.

He could never have asked a stranger where the toilets were – he was painfully shy and, apart from George and, eventually, his uncles, he had a pathological terror of men that he can only ascribe to his Somerleyton Road cot experience. Once, not long after his adoption,

Margaret caught him hiding in the coal hole with a group photograph and a pair of scissors stabbing and cutting at the faces of all the men.

Nowadays these incidents would be taken extremely seriously, reported to doctors and addressed sympathetically and with therapy, but in the early fifties such behaviour was seen either as something childish that would be 'grown out of' or as an inbred character fault. Embarrassed parents kept quiet, did the best they could and carried on regardless, while the world stood at a distance with arms folded, watched and judged.

In this ignorant and unforgiving world, at the age of five and wearing his pink-rimmed NHS glasses, Clive Jackson started school and began what he describes – amazingly considering what came later – as "the worst time of my life".

*

The Grove Vale School experience began well. Even in those days his memory was unusually good and his first teacher, Miss Jane, would call him up to the front of the class to entertain the other children by retelling George and Margaret's bed-time stories. Since he was inclined to attention-seeking behaviour and felt safe among women and other children, he loved this. Here he got his first inkling that knowledge and information were to be found in books and looked forward to the time when he would be able to read them and learn for himself. Miss Jane told his parents that she thought he might grow up to be a writer.

Such favour from authority does not make for popularity, and when the other children began to progress in their reading and he did not, the bullies had all the ammunition they needed. Long days were spent puzzling over the incomprehensible squiggles in his books and on the blackboard, and being jeered at by his classmates. Those days often ended with the gang waiting for him and attacking him on his way home, smashing his glasses so that the next day he could not even see what he was supposed to be reading.

Sympathetic Miss Jane was replaced by less understanding teachers who, while coping with unruly classes of forty-five and more, had little time or inclination to give special attention to Clive. Naturally left-handed, he was forced to try to write with his 'right' hand and punished for reverting to the 'wrong' one. To make things worse, like Joyce, figures and mathematics were as much a mystery to him as reading and writing. On one occasion a teacher made a show of stalking to his desk to stab a pencil into his maths book and score it deeply across before throwing it across the room. Gleefully the bullies took note and did the same as often as they could. When he thinks back to this time, the fear is almost as real to him now as it was then.

Clive had no idea why he could not do what came so easily to everyone else – he just knew he couldn't help it, however much other people seemed to think he could, and that he was intelligent, however much other people believed otherwise. The term, 'Dyslexia' was unheard of in those days – there were only labels like 'illiterate', 'stupid', 'lazy' and 'bad'. This was the era of the dunce's cap, of being sent to stand in the corner, the era when public humiliation, sarcasm and condemnation was expected to produce positive results, when bullying was effectively encouraged as salutary or 'character-forming'. This was the era when left-handedness was seen as a character flaw to be eradicated, when a seven-year-old who could not grasp letters and figures could be relegated to the baby class and forced to sit on a baby chair with his knees up under his chin. This was the era when 'persistently refusing to learn' could mean being sent to the headmistress and beaten with a slipper.

All this happened to Clive and could be at least partially excused as being customary and acceptable at the time. The actions of one of Clive's female teachers would have been deemed unacceptable in any day and age. Baffled once again, through a combination of poor eyesight and lack of reading ability, by what was on the blackboard, he took his exercise book up to the front of the class and asked her to explain it to him. As he stood by her side, looking down with her at his book on her desk, he felt her free hand slide up his leg and inside his shorts, where she fondled him.

The reaction of his body was instant – the first time anything like this had ever happened to him. Without anything being said he knew this was a secret, that she should not be doing this to him, but that he liked it. He may not have learned how to read fluently, write legibly or add up accurately at school but he soon learned how to deceive, how to conceal and how to lie.

Not long after, a neighbour – a man in his twenties – offered to take him to the swings and sexually assaulted him in the toilets there. Confused about what was happening to him and whether it was good or bad, once again he said nothing about it to anyone. The Bible warns against stirring up adult sensations at an inappropriately early age (*Song of Solomon 2:7 and 3:5*) and these premature experiences sowed seeds that would bring a bleak harvest for Clive in later years.

Home, by contrast, was his sanctuary of warmth and love. He had a particularly strong bond with Margaret's mother, who he called Nana, and who took him shopping with her and bought him the toy cars he liked to play with. One evening a family party was held at Archdale Road and Clive aged around six, was in bed upstairs. His Nana was going to come in and sit with him so a chair was brought in for her and put beside his bed. Nana hid two bottles of Guinness under the chair "for later" which she told him to keep secret. After a while, George and Margaret came in to see them and Margaret handed her mother two bottles of Guinness “for later”. Clive obediently kept quiet about the two already under the chair.

Throughout the party nearly every aunt and uncle popped in to say hello to Clive and nearly every one brought a bottle of Guinness for Nana who accepted them all with the same innocent gratitude and added them to her stash. As the evening wore on, the stories she read to Clive from his big blue book of nursery tales became somewhat confused and frequently ran into each other! Eventually Nana asked Clive to come and sit on the chair so she could have “a bit of a lie down” on his bed. Sometime later when George and Margaret returned, they found Nana fast asleep on the bed, her head pillowed on her grandson’s shoulder, Clive in his pyjamas on the chair with his arm around her and a pile of empties on the floor. “Shh,” he cautioned them, “Nana’s tired and she’s just having a little sleep; I’m looking after her...”

He was eight when one day he was accosted by a woman outside the school gate. She came from Peckham and her son Laurence was a classmate of Clive’s – they had played together in the street as toddlers back in the Somerleyton Road days. She always came to collect Laurence, while Clive lived close enough to the school to walk home alone. Today she couldn’t wait to speak to him.

“Your mother’s dead,” she said.

“My mother’s at home,” Clive replied, confused. The woman shook her head impatiently.

“No, your real mother,” she told him. “She put her head in the oven and gassed herself.”

Only she knew why she thought an eight-year-old needed this information or how she expected him to react to it. As it was, he obeyed his first instinct and ran all the way home to Archdale Road, bursting in through the door. "You're not my real mother," he informed Margaret breathlessly, "my real mother's dead." She was more angry than he could ever remember seeing her – but with Laurence's mother and not with him.

In a way he could never have articulated, it was fundamentally important to him that Margaret was his 'real' mother and George his father, because it was the certainties and stability of the Jackson household to which he clung like a life-raft in a stormy sea. At the end of her tether, his mother might say, "You'd make an angel from heaven swear!" but she nursed him tenderly through the measles that threatened the sight of his left eye. Together she and George helped him deal with the pain and incomprehension of what had happened to Joyce.

So terrified was he of losing all this that when they asked him if he might like a brother – maybe with a second adoption in mind – he told them in no uncertain terms that he would not. When all the world was against him, home was where he was unconditionally accepted, and he had no intention of sharing it – or his parents' love and attention – with anyone else.

For the Jacksons even to be considering taking on another boy is a testament to the triumph of hope over experience – they had more than enough on their hands as it was. Like many victims of bullying, Clive was very susceptible to overtures of apparent friendship, however damaging they might prove. One day a twelve-year old boy from a neighbouring street took him on a bus to

Camberwell Green Woolworths, dodging the fare, and showed him how easy it was to shoplift pencils and chocolate.

One of Clive's clearest memories is of himself in school uniform sitting in a bombed-out church eating the stolen chocolates and how they tasted better than any chocolates he had ever had before. No punitive lightning bolt from heaven hit him and no policeman's heavy hand landed on his shoulder. He was hooked on the adrenaline-rush of theft and, worse, he had lost the instinctive deterrent of fear that had kept him on the straight and narrow so far. From then on, nothing was safe from him that wasn't nailed down and he was caught many times at school, but no amount of punishment outweighed the 'kick' he got from doing it.

Other 'friends', finding he could be dared into almost anything, had great fun egging him on to more and more outrageous stunts, then running away and leaving him to take the consequences. This culminated in him setting off a street-corner fire alarm and then, finding himself abandoned as usual, going quietly home and saying nothing about it, only to find two massive fire engines outside the house soon after! In those days there was a five pound fine for improper use of the fire alarm – a considerable sum for a not-especially-well-off household.

Many fathers would have considered draconian punishment to be in order and well deserved. George took his son with him to Peckham Fire Station the next day and let him see the fine being paid, and then the two of them went on a tour of the station, inspected all the engines and even saw a crew rushing out on a ‘shout’. Instead of the Fire Brigade being ‘the enemy’, they were now a source of awe and respect, and the young Clive had a far better understanding of why he should not waste their time.

George himself was always up for a laugh and not above a bit of minor mischief of his own. Clive well remembers the family party where his father and uncles 'acquired' the cover of a Belisha beacon and used it as a giant punchbowl! There were a lot of parties amongst the extended family, all with much joy and laughter and taking place at the various houses of his uncles and aunts. Clive particularly remembers his Aunty Flo's house with its big Victorian rooms and high ceilings, perhaps because it was so much more spacious than Archdale road, which did not even have a bathroom. The local swimming pool also housed the local baths – big tubs where people could bathe at a shilling a time, calling out "more hot for number six!" or "more cold!" at which the attendant would let either hot or cold water in from the outside. On one occasion, queuing for the Brill Cream dispenser after their baths, George and Clive had to instruct a foreign man that it was for use on his hair, and not his face!

Walking home from a get-together at Flo's house one evening, George became alarmed. "I think the alcohol must have gone to my feet," he told his wife and son. "They've swollen up; my shoes are killing me." He removed his shoes and hobbled home in his socks, finding every stone on the path with cries of "ouch!" to the not-very sympathetic laughter of his family! Next day, still worried, he went back to Flo's house and described the problem to Uncle Pat, who had also returned. "Your feet haven't swollen," Pat told him, "Those are my shoes! I went home last night in yours, wondering why my feet had shrunk..."

It was fun-loving George who, though not a churchgoer himself, instilled in his son a respect for God and gave him a glimpse of deeper certainties that would one day prove an even more reliable bedrock in even stormier waters. During holidays, particularly on the Isle of Sheppey, Clive became fascinated with churches and the glorious beauty of the stained glass windows. For him there was always something compelling about the light. His father happily took him into every one they saw, explaining the history and the significance of them.

Clive remembers the impact Canterbury Cathedral and especially the tomb of the Black Prince had on him the first time he saw them. He began to ponder a lot about the cross and the crucifixion, going into different churches, removing his cap and sitting gazing at the multi-coloured light coming through the windows and asking Jesus in his head: 'Who are You?' and 'Where are You?' Slowly, Christ began to seep into his soul.

He asked his father for a book of Bible stories and, with the rudimentary reading ability he had managed to acquire, began to learn about the Man of Sorrows, scorned, rejected and attacked, and to identify with Him. A deep yearning to visit Israel developed and endured; he began to attend his local East Dulwich Church, St John's, took confirmation classes and, at the age of eleven, was duly confirmed.

Two

Counterattack

The evening sun glows golden on the brickwork of the church. Not long rebuilt after being bombed in the war, it serves as a symbol of renewal and victory to the community, even those who only ever enter its doors to be 'hatched, matched and dispatched'. Tonight those doors are ajar and the sound of music seeps out – it is the bands' regular practice night.

The boy does not use the main entrance, but slips quietly round the side and into the vestry. The music is louder here, covering any sound he might make. For several minutes he stands in the middle of the cluttered room, revolving slowly and peering at the choir robes, piles of hymnals, paperwork, half-burned candles and dust. Then he smiles. Walking to the battered metal filing cabinet he pulls open a draw and thrusts a hand in, under the row of files, right to the back. When he pulls it put again, it is clutching a cash box. Minutes later he leaves the church, the box back in its place considerably lighter, his pockets heavy and bulging.

From just inside the church porch, his eyes full of sadness and his lips moving in prayer, the vicar watches him go.

*

The devil doesn't like losing people, particularly such promising material as Clive. The boy's imperfect understanding of his own unearned salvation made him a prime target for temptation, misinformation and attack. His brief moment of walking in the light was followed almost immediately by eclipse, and this time the darkness was to endure for many years.

Clive's stealing was becoming more of a compulsion than a habit. He stole from everywhere except his own home – that was where he buried the money in the garden. Later he would unearth it and use it to go up to Kensington by cab and visit all the major museums and galleries. Desperate for knowledge and unable to get any at school, he told himself he was funding his own education and so buying himself a future.

Even St John's wasn't safe from his depredations – he regularly hung round the vestry there and stole money belonging to the band. Whatever ingenious hiding places the Reverend Targett used to hide his cash box, Clive seemed to have a sixth sense of where to find it. He salved his conscience by always leaving a little money behind and by using some of it to buy flowers and chocolates for the vicar's teenage daughter, whom he admired.

His interest in God and beauty had altered subtly into a morbid obsession with death and the afterlife. He began to paint pictures – mostly of quaint cottages – in colour if he was in a happy mood or, more and more often, in unrelieved black if he was not.

George and Margaret were deeply worried about him and went to see the Reverend Targett, as the vicar of Clive's church, to consult him about their son's stealing and ask his advice as to what they should do about it. They were horrified to hear that he had been stealing from the church as well, and this meeting between parents and vicar effectively ended Clive's association with St John's.

His fascination with death, however, persisted. One day George came into his son's bedroom to find him with a ligature around his neck, seriously attempting to strangle himself, in an attempt to find out 'what it felt like to die'. This episode led to his doctor becoming involved and a referral to the Maudsley psychiatric hospital for assessment. He remembers various sensors being stuck to his head and readings taken on his first visit but after that he settled into a routine of weekly interviews with the child psychologist – a pattern that was to go on for some considerable time.

Clive very much enjoyed these sessions. They got him time off from the hated school and he was the undisputed centre of attention – just as he liked it. He lapped up all the prop-based tests featuring bricks and the drawing of pictures, cheerfully lied through his teeth during the interviews and generally wrapped the doctors around his little finger.

When the therapist had finished with him for the day he would wander around the hospital stealing unattended money from patients and staff alike. During this time he left Grove Vale behind him – with much relief on both sides – and moved up to William Penn School and the world of secondary education.

His reputation had preceded him. He was put straight into 3 Manual Class, denoting that, when he left school at the age of fourteen, he would be a manual labourer and there was no real point attempting to teach him anything more. Clive just did not see himself in this light – he *knew* he was an intelligent boy who appreciated art and was cleverer than most – clever enough to bamboozle the doctors at the Maudsley – but his inability to read or add up said otherwise.

Bullying at William Penn was as bad, if not worse, than at Grove Vale, but it was here that Clive abandoned his customary passivity and first began to stand up for himself. A boy called Wingate, the leader of a gang of bullies, took a particular exception to him and he knew it was only a matter of time before a serious attack occurred. He spent his lunchtimes practising boxing with the sports master. When the gang cornered him in the boy's toilets egging Wingate on to beat him up, he knew, however terrified he was, he had to do something now, so he delivered his best right hook straight to Wingate's nose. The bully went reeling, blood pouring from his face. The gang melted away in consternation and from that day on he had no more bullying problems at William Penn.

He had attended 'big school' for almost a year when the Maudsley finally washed its hands of him and advised his parents to report him to the police and have him prosecuted for his stealing. The Jacksons did no such thing. They, alone of all people, understood that he was damaged and could not help himself – though even they did not know how deep the damage ran. As much as he was capable of loving anyone, Clive loved George and Margaret and he knew how much his behaviour hurt them. To spare them any more pain, he asked if he could be sent to a boarding school for the remaining year of his school life and, with the agreement of all concerned, he was enrolled at Coombe Hall School for maladjusted boys at East Grinstead.

Coombe Hall was a place of bewildering contrasts and extremes – on one hand a pit of depravity populated by a horde of minimally supervised hormonal delinquents – on the other a place where responsibility was encouraged and Clive finally began to grow up. To begin with, though, he was plunged into an atmosphere where both violence and homosexual behaviour were customary, day and night, both in the dormitories and in the grounds.

Still wetting the bed every night and confused about his sexuality ever since the incident in the park toilets, he entered into the prevailing mood of the place. He formed relationships with other boys and created his own fantasy world where he was hiding out from a gang of London criminals who were 'after him' and might turn up looking for him – might be concealed in the grounds of the school waiting to ambush him and kill him for what he 'knew' about them. Staff and fellow pupils were either half-convinced by his tales or bestowed much time and attention on him trying to reassure him he was mistaken.

Two things happened that turned the tide. A boy called Butterworth, whose main claim to fame was having beheaded all the school geese with a spade, enticed him into a toilet cubicle and perpetrated an assault on him that convinced him beyond all doubt that he was not homosexual. The second was the inter-school Dewar Shield swimming competition where he won a great victory for the school, much to the delight of the headmaster and everyone else at Coombe Hall.

He was awarded a medal for that, his self esteem blossomed and, one morning he woke up to find his sheets were dry for the first time ever. Given the responsibility of being head of the dormitory he discovered he had unexpected leadership skills. Even the stealing diminished to a trickle – though he still could not resist overwhelming temptation when it was in front of him. At the age of fourteen, he left school for good and returned to live at Archdale Road with his parents.

As foreseen, his inadequacy in the areas of reading, writing and adding up severely curtailed his choice of jobs. Over the next year he changed jobs frequently working as, amongst other things, a builder's labourer, a laundry lorry attendant and a plumber's mate, always looking for something better, but hampered by his inability to measure, calculate or fill in time sheets.

The worst job he remembers doing involved standing beneath a chute in a wood yard and filling sacks with the sawdust and shavings that poured down it – he just was not quick enough at changing each full sack for the next empty one. At Coombe Hall he had heard other boys talk about joining the army and it seemed like a good idea to him, but for that he had to be seventeen and a half. Until then he had to make a living and at least labouring jobs paid well – £14 per week was a good wage for a young lad in 1960.

Clive was determined to make something of himself and earn his own self-respect. Despite the thieving he knew himself to be fundamentally honest, in the same way as he knew himself to be intelligent despite what others saw as evidence to the contrary. The thieving was like something imposed on him from outside; a habit he didn't like and which made him and his family deeply unhappy. During this time he had no contact with any church and so no Spiritual guidance about temptation and resisting it. But he still had Christ within him.

There came a day during his stint as plumber's mate when Arthur, the plumber, left him to finish a job while he went off to start another. Before he left he told Clive that the lady of the house had lost a £90 diamond earring down the drain. Alone, Clive opened out a wire coat hanger, formed a hook on the end and put it down the drain turning it about and trying to hook the earring. By a million to one chance he succeeded and managed to manoeuvre it all the way to the top, and he remembers still the sight of the massive diamond glittering on his palm and the thought of the riches it would bring him.

When Arthur returned and asked "Any luck?" Clive hesitated and then chose to hand the earring over. It was a momentous decision and it kept him crime-free for some years to come.

His visits to museums and art galleries were now honestly funded and he still enjoyed his trips into town to soak up the culture. He was particularly struck by a sculpture of three female nudes at the Tate Gallery; they were his first sight of naked women and he stood entranced, gazing at the sculpture for some time. Later, at Brixton Skating Rink he saw their flesh and blood (but clothed!) equivalent; a beautiful girl his own age, tall and slim with long blonde hair, and fell heavily and hopelessly in love.

On the face of it Sheila was way out of his league – a professional model, who had been presented with an award for being Beauty Queen of Lambeth by Roger Moore, but the attraction was mutual from the moment he got her attention by snatching her scarf as he skated by. Clive was back in the building trade by then and spent his days doing menial tasks black with grime, but with his girl on his arm, he felt like a million dollars.

Under her influence he began to take an interest in his appearance outside working hours, adopting mod fashion and Italian suits. His mother couldn't get him out of the bathroom (George had installed one at Archdale Road by this time) and he reeked of Brut. It was the heady days of the early sixties when teenagers felt that the world belonged to them and nothing was impossible. Clive began to paint pictures again and listen to classical music on his parents' radiogram – to feel like a proper person with a place in society like everyone else.

Sheila's father, a former prisoner of war of the Japanese, got on well with Clive, although her mother didn't like him at all. George and Margaret were overjoyed at the new stability and happiness in his life and, somewhat rashly, granted the young couple the private use of the front room at Archdale Road – a privilege they took full, if naive advantage of. Clive remembers his father walking in unexpectedly one evening to find them both sitting naked in front of the fire and asking wryly "What's the matter, too hot for you?" Later he took his son aside and told him to bear in mind that any resulting pregnancy would be Clive's own responsibility. Two weeks later it became apparent that the advice was already too late.

The sixties might be swinging but a baby outside marriage, especially in such a very young girl, was still a matter for scandal and secrecy and Sheila was packed off to Littlehampton to see out the pregnancy and birth well away from Brixton. Clive started a new job as a roofer's labourer, even more determined both to join the army and marry Sheila as soon as he was old enough. After the birth, their daughter, Deborah, remained at Littlehampton in the nursery until she was deemed old enough for Sheila to bring home and take charge of. During this time, Clive and Sheila went together to visit her every weekend and learn to care for her. In between, Sheila resumed her modelling career. The flat in Electric Avenue where she lived with her parents was hardly family-friendly; it was on the top floor and everything – shopping and baby included, had to be carried up eighty steps.

At the end of 1963, having reached the magic age of seventeen-and-a-half, Clive headed for Whitehall to join up. National Service had come to an end in 1960 and the Cold War was in full swing. A strong professional army to stand against the

Russians and stop them overrunning Europe was seen as an urgent requirement and volunteers were welcomed with open arms. His less than perfect eyesight precluded him from anything but infantry regiments, but his failure of the written entrance exam was no barrier at all – they told him optimistically that he could learn his maths and English as a soldier. He was duly inducted into the Royal Fusiliers, also known as the City of London Regiment, and packed off to Sutton Coldfield for basic training. Deborah was, by then, a year old.

From the first he took to the army like a duck to water. Here was the structure, the stability, the sense of belonging he had been looking for all his life. Here he could actually do what was required of him, and do it well. He excelled at physical training, at long cross-country runs, at weapons training, even at cleaning his kit. Reading books might still be beyond him, but he could read maps with no trouble at all. No longer was he bottom of the class at everything – here he was better than others at several things, and his self-esteem rose proportionately. The one thing he wasn't keen on was boxing, but that was compulsory.

Every blue sky has a cloud and, in every institutional situation of this sort, there is always a bully. The Sutton Coldfield bully made it known to everyone that he wanted to get in the ring with Clive at the forthcoming boxing tournament because he hated him and wanted to give him a pasting. Clive was afraid but well-versed in hiding his fear – he also remembered how he had successfully defended himself back at William Penn. When, either by accident or design, he did find himself facing the bully across the boxing ring he knew his only hope was to go in fast and hard. At the first ding of the bell he shot across the canvas and landed the same mighty punch as before, right on his opponent's nose. The fight was stopped there and then and he had no more trouble.

Basic training continued with a trip to Wales for his first sight of mountains, and finished with Clive awarded the temporary rank of Sergeant and given the responsibility of leading the rest of the recruits to their posting at Osnabrück Barracks in Germany. Their departure was filmed by the BBC and his proud parents were able to watch him go up the ramp at RAF Lyneham and into the plane. Before he went, he had telephoned Sheila and asked her to marry him and she had said yes. Even though the first instruction he was given on arrival by the

Company Sergeant Major was "Get those stripes off!" he was content.

The army's confidence that they could have him fluent in reading and adding up was predictably misplaced, but there were plenty of other things he could excel at; cycle-racing, speed-skating, swimming – he tried them all. He still remembers his delight and astonishment at coming in the top three of a cross country race of 1000 men. He also achieved proficiency to the level of marksman in several different weapons, since each one mastered meant a raise in pay.

He and Sheila had married while he was on leave at the age of 18 and they were waiting for married quarters to become available so they could be reunited and begin family life with Deborah. It would be a long wait. In the mean time he became involved in drama, acting in a play alongside Leslie Grantham –

later the East Enders actor – who was stationed there at the same time. The play was about the Battle of Waterloo and Clive played a ghost returned from the battle.

Spiritually, this time was a total desert. As opposed to Christ as he had once been attracted, Clive refused to attend Church Parades as a gesture of rebellion and non-conformity aimed as much at God as at the authorities. It was a pattern that was to recur throughout his life and one that made him a sitting duck for the forces of darkness but, sure of him, the devil left him alone for the time being.

God, Whose mercy and grace are deeper than anything, never did.

Three

Battlefield

In a flat in Osnabrück Barracks, West Germany, two men and a woman are sitting round a table. The couple who live there have just entertained their friend to dinner and the evening stretches out before them. They have no television, only a radio with diminishing reception at this late hour, a record player and a few records. Conversation becomes desultory and then lapses.

"Here," the guest says at last. "Let me show you a Victorian parlour game – this is how they used to entertain themselves in the evenings in the olden days. Have you got a mirror? That's right; lay it flat on the table. And an empty wine glass? Now we'll need twenty-six bits of paper to write the alphabet on and put them

round the edge – oh, and two more – write 'Yes' on one and 'No' on the other; they go one at each end. That's great. Now put the glass upside down on the mirror.

"Do you know what this is called? It's called a Ouija Board. You can ask the spirits questions and get answers. It's just a bit of fun – something to pass the time. Nothing serious – it'll be a laugh. So what do you want to ask, Clive? Come on – there must be something you've always wanted to know..."

*

The British Army on the Rhine in the sixties and seventies was part of NATO's buffer against the very real threat of a Russian invasion of Europe. It was the time of the Vietnam War and the Bay of Pigs, and the authorities were concerned enough to ask the soldiers whether they would be 'loyal in the event of a communist government' an extraordinary question that suggests they might have been making plans for 'the resistance' well in advance of any possible need.

Like most of his contemporaries, Clive had no interest in politics and only a vague idea of the 'red menace' he was there to combat. Being a new soldier to the unit was not always a barrel of laughs – most of them slept with machetes under their pillows to deter initiation attacks by the more seasoned troops. The practice of 'bed-railing' involved creeping up on a youngster fast asleep in his dormitory, removing the iron bar 'foot board' of the bed and hitting him over the head with it.

Clive remembers waking once to find a soldier standing over him with the rail of his bed held high, just about to bring it down on him, and informing him, “If I survive, when I get out of hospital I will kill you!” Possibly having heard about the Sutton Coldfield boxing match, his would-be assailant thought better of it, lowered the bed-rail harmlessly and left.

On the whole, though, Clive was enjoying life, participating in exercises and manoeuvres as far afield as the Mediterranean, Norway and the Arctic Circle, training against biological and nuclear threats, delegating to conceal his lack of literacy and numeracy as much as possible. Once, while stationed at the Europa Point Barracks in Gibraltar, he heard a tremendous roar and looked out across the Strait to see two large and powerful speedboats racing past at top speed. He later found out that these had been ordered by Israel from a

French boat builder in Marseilles, a place with strong connections to the Jewish nation. Subsequent sanctions against Israel had caused the French authorities to withhold the boats, so a 'specialist Israeli unit' had been sent to 'liberate' them. Clive was the only man at the barracks to see them on their way home.

The army was always a world of leg-pulls and tricks – some of them quite elaborate. Clive remembers how he and his comrades used to get revenge on stroppy fellow-soldiers, who would be plied with drink until they fell into bed in a deep sleep, then transferred, still tucked in their bedclothes, to a specific point on the runway of the airfield. The jokers would then wait at a safe distance and laugh as the ashen-faced victim sat bolt upright to find a plane taking off over his head.

One pair of twins were so desperate to get out of the army they set fire to the Osnabrück fuel compound. Jerry cans of petrol exploded and shot sixty feet into the night sky, while all the soldiers hung out of the barracks windows cheering each one. The twins didn't get themselves expelled for this, but later achieved it by shutting a man in a steel locker and throwing him out of a second floor window. He survived the experience and the twins repeated the stunt every weekend (not with the same man!) until the authorities finally had enough of them.

After a year, Sheila and Deborah came out to Germany and the Jackson family moved into a block of army flats a short bus ride from the barracks. Clive had been leading the life of a single man in the meantime and he was not quite ready yet to give that up, but on the whole he was feeling happy and secure and that he had a place in the world where he mattered. It was wonderful to have Sheila there and what she didn't know about, he thought, couldn't hurt her.

Unfortunately it is impossible to cheat without lying. And lying – always a weakness of Clive's – is an open invitation to the Father of Lies. The devil was already exploiting Clive's sexual weakness – putting temptation in his way and watching him fall for it – now he moved in on another area of vulnerability, Clive's desperate thirst for knowledge and his feeling of aggrieved injustice that he couldn't acquire it because he couldn't read properly when everyone else could.

So David came to dinner and introduced the Jacksons to his 'Victorian parlour game.' What Clive was being offered now was not just the common knowledge anyone could get by reading books – this was 'deeper knowledge'; knowledge hidden even to people who could read – and knowledge is power. In the beginning, under the fruit tree in Eden, the devil dangled knowledge and power in front of Eve (*Genesis 3:4-6*) and it worked so well he's never had to change the formula since.

Neither of the Jacksons ever really thought of the Ouija Board as 'a bit of fun'. For Sheila it was spooky and disconcerting and, when it correctly predicted the gender and birth-date of their second child, Christopher, she bailed out all together and would have nothing more to do with it. For Clive it very soon became an obsession, the feeling of power and excitement it gave him far exceeding the buzz he'd got from stealing and he soon found he couldn't do without it. He introduced other soldiers to the practice, including SAS men, and has since often wondered what they did with it.

All this time he tried hard to believe he was doing what he did 'in the Name of God'. Despite his outward opposition he had never really stopped believing: "Jesus," he says, "was always there at the back of my mind." If he could have read the Bible properly, or had consulted a minister, he would have known that God forbade what he was doing, and with good reason, but he did not know and was careful not to ask.

One night, returning on foot to base he saw his first apparition. There was no night-vision equipment in those days, so walking in the dark really was walking in the dark. The figure appeared like smoke or dry ice, edged with a hard, silver-coloured band that glowed inwards rather than outwards. He remembers that he was not remotely afraid and that it stayed with him until he reached the entrance to the base, when he turned to find it gone.

Other visitations followed. In a cottage in the Lake District with a local girlfriend and an Australian couple he got out the board and all four clearly saw the shadow of a Catholic cardinal in his round hat and with a hooked nose. The other three who had thought they were merely playing a game reacted with astonished fear, but Clive was exhilarated. During a brief posting to the Middle East, the board told him something invisible was standing next to him. An onlooker scoffed "prove it!" so Clive instructed the being, through the board, to touch the man's leg, which it did, scaring the former sceptic into terrified flight.

These incidents could have been the top of a slippery slope to ever-deeper occult involvement, had not God intervened. Clive was, after all, still stubbornly insisting that he was operating 'in the Name of God' – and the Name of God is a mighty weapon, even misused in the hands of the ignorant. Out here in the desert, he felt a renewal of the powerful urge he'd once had to get to Israel, to see Jerusalem and to walk in the footsteps of Christ. His eyes were opened and his self-delusion demolished. He realised that he loved God and Jesus, and that what he was doing was wrong. Returning to England, he gave up using the Ouija Board.

He still didn't really understand what he had been dabbling with and had no idea about spiritual warfare, and no concept of the battle that had been raging over him all his life. He really thought he was strong enough to put all his occult activities behind him and walk away with no backlash. He knew now that he loved God, but he didn't know that love, on its own and without complete, committed surrender, is not enough (*James 4:7-8*). Posted to the Joint Services Outdoor Pursuits Centre in Towyn, Wales, Sheila and the children joined him and they made what they fondly believed would be a fresh start.

*

At first all went well – it seemed the perfect placement for Clive with his love of sport and physical pastimes. He threw himself into all the activities – went fell-running, took up mountaineering and he was even shortlisted to climb Everest, though he did not make the final team. Towyn was on the coast, so the children had the beach to enjoy, and Clive often took them on family outings further afield.

Once in a café all the family had decided on faggots and chips (not the oversized, frozen meatballs of today – proper traditional faggots made from minced cuts of pork, seasoned and enclosed in something like a sausage skin) but the young Christopher went very quiet when his arrived. Eventually he informed everyone, "I don't like these maggots; they are covered in plastic!" Having never heard of faggots, he had been expecting the maggots he was familiar with from fishing expeditions, and evidently had no concerns about eating those for his dinner, but plastic-wrapped meat was another matter...

The game of happy families didn't last. Deprived by his own choice of the illicit excitement of the Ouija board, Clive began subconsciously to look for something else. Given the chance, Christ would have filled the gap but, unlike his dealings with the devil, his love of Christ was a closely guarded secret, suppressed for fear of ridicule – the approval of his fellow men was very important to Clive. Unsurprising then, that it was the drinking that got to him first – drinking to excess is, of course, an army tradition and expected of soldiers by their peers, but to someone with his addictive personality it was a dangerous hobby.

Then there were the women – good-looking as he was and with a warm engaging personality there would always be women – and with the women came the necessity of lying, and close behind the lying came the theft. Given his foothold (*Ephesians 4:26-27*) the devil took full use of it. In early 1974, George became very ill with cancer. After his retirement, he and Margaret had moved to West Kingsdown in Kent, and it was there he was admitted to hospital for what was likely to be the last time. Clive applied for and got compassionate leave to go and visit him for the weekend.

Boxing was, in those days, compulsory for soldiers – men were paired off and expected to fight each other. Clive had never really liked boxing despite the two occasions when a well-aimed punch had got him out of trouble, but he was a tall, strong and very fit, and that Friday he was put in the ring with a sergeant from Lesotho, another powerful man. A chance blow to Clive's head damaged the muscles supporting his left eye causing the eyeball to retract into his head. He was taken at once to Cambridge military hospital where he was operated on. He woke up the next day with double vision which has never entirely left him despite his being told it would clear in a couple of weeks.

Desperate to get to George, he left the hospital before he was really well enough to do so and travelled to Kent, where he met Margaret at George's bedside. She was about to wash her husband but he stopped her; "Let Clive do it," he said. So Clive took a cloth and washed his father's face, arms and hands. After the visit he went back with Margaret to his parents' bungalow and spent the night there. George died early the next morning.

A distraught Margaret, jealous of that last wash and the closeness between father and son that had never lessened through all Clive's troubles, shrugged off his proffered comfort and would not have his arm around her. It brought home to him that he had lost his one and only source of utterly unconditional love. He kissed George's cold forehead and thanked God for him and all he had done and been. A major anchor point –

maybe the major anchor point – in his tempestuous life was gone.

Losing his adoptive father had much the same effect on him that losing his biological father must have had on Joyce. Nothing seemed to matter anymore and, hovering on the brink of mental illness, he abandoned all restraint. There came a day when Clive was out on an expedition with an officer and some other soldiers and could not resist stealing an ice-axe and a jumper from a shop. The officer, maybe already suspicious, saw him, and he was arrested, charged and arraigned for a Court Martial. Suddenly it hit him, with the force of a moving vehicle, that he had thrown away everything of worth that he had managed to build up for himself. Desperately ashamed, he felt that he would never be free of these destructive behaviour patterns and that they would rule and ruin his life forever.

He broke down completely, and was found on Towyn beach, lying in the sand as though crucified. The Court Martial was abandoned and he was transferred instead to the Joint Armed Services Psychiatric Unit at Netley Military Hospital, Southampton, where he spent some periods in a padded cell. When his family came to visit he recognised Sheila but did not know his own children. Furious at what had happened and blaming God, he remembered that the Bible said man cannot look at the sun (*Job 37:31*), so he made a point of staring at it in defiance and was fortunate not to damage his sight.

Deep inside he knew that God was not to blame for his actions and neither, really, was the devil. He, Clive Jackson, had chosen to do these things and his anger with God was really just projection of his anger with himself. With the abrupt change of mood characteristic of the bipolar he lapsed into dangerous self-condemnation. All he could think was that he had lost his beloved father, lost his career, his family – lost everything; and that he had failed as a husband and father, as a man. As a soldier, he had seen no active service despite a short stint in Northern Ireland – he could not even die for his country. He decided to die anyway, took razor blades outside to a summer house in the grounds and slashed one wrist before he was stopped. It took seven men to get him back into the hospital and sedated.

When he woke up it was a beautiful morning, his wrist had been stitched and the birds were singing – for a few moments he was glad he was alive, but the feeling did not last. At the age of twenty-eight he was medically discharged from the army and went to live with Sheila and the children in a council flat she had taken in Woking to be near to her parents who now lived in Byfleet.

There was no specific diagnosis – this was the early seventies when the term 'mentally ill' covered a multitude of conditions and carried the stigma of the worst of them. Unemployed, depressed and on medication that he did not always take properly, he slid back into his womanising and drinking ways and became verbally aggressive and utterly unreasonable. Sheila, who had always loved him more than he loved her, who had stuck faithfully by him, home and abroad, through all the misery, came finally to the end of her tether. She and her mother had the police evict him from the flat – he was in such a frenzied state they brought a net to throw over him like a wild animal – and then she filed for divorce.

For some time he existed in a series of rented rooms, his mind vague and fuzzy, either due to his medication or to drink or to a combination of both. From the age of three he had been used to being surrounded by people – the Jackson clan, the army, his own family – and he had difficulty coping with being alone. Long ago, after the childhood abuse had awakened in him an unhealthy obsession with sex, he had become addicted to pornography and also formed the habit of voyeurism, often leaving his Archdale road home at night to prowl the Dulwich streets in search of uncurtained windows and courting couples. Now he did the same in Woking.

Four

Ambush

The guide gestures at the view. "This is where Jesus was warned that the fox, King Herod, wanted to kill Him. This is where the feet of our Lord stood when He looked at Jerusalem and mourned it as the place that stoned the prophets and refused to be gathered beneath His wings. This is the very place!"

Clive is where he has always wanted to be, where he has dreamed of being nearly all his life – where Jesus was, walking where He walked. Israel. And now he is here it is hot and crowded, and the woman by his side is slightly bored, and yes, it is impressive, but... What was he expecting? What did he come here to find? Whatever it was, it still eludes him. This should have been the crowning experience of his life; instead it is leaving him mildly disappointed; unfulfilled. Thirsty.

"Come on," he says to his companion. "Let's go and get a drink."

*

Jesus knows where every sparrow falls and still more where every one of His people fall (*Matthew 10:29-31*), and He never takes back the hand He holds out to them, however long it is before they accept it, and whatever they choose to do in the meantime. After a while, Clive was drawn inexorably back to church, began to attend Emmanuel Chapel in Woking and found two supportive Christian brothers there called Jim and Chris. One day he was walking with Jim past the Woking Centre Pool (the site is now occupied by ToysRUs in the

Peacock Shopping Centre) and Jim suggested he went in, presented his army life-saving qualifications and asked for a job as a life guard.

Nothing could have been less likely to succeed. True, he was a qualified life guard with certificates to prove it, but he was massively overweight due to his medication and lifestyle, and a mess in almost every other way as well. But God was in the suggestion as He was in the suggester. Clive went in, saw the manager, explained his situation truthfully – a miracle in itself – and told him that he had been a soldier. By a million-to-one chance, the manager was also ex-army – in fact he had been a Quarter Master Sergeant Instructor at a forces PT school. Out of army solidarity he gave Clive a job as a life guard.

The return of a structure to his life worked wonders. He determined that he was going to make the best of this opportunity – to start with he was going to train, as he had been taught in the army. He began to swim every day, gradually building up the time and distance. Army life had left him with a basic fitness underneath all the flab; the excess weight dropped off and he was soon swimming a mile in twenty-five minutes. His confidence in himself increased.

The manager had no reason to regret his altruism in employing Clive. One day, sitting on the side of the pool, Clive looked towards the deep end and saw just a pair of hands above the water, slowly disappearing from sight. He dived in and retrieved an elderly man from the bottom of the pool, hauling him up the ladder and out onto the tiles. He then performed CPR while the man's wife lamented from the balcony that he was eighty and should never have been in there, and always thought he could do more than was the case. The man lived – hopefully taking more care of himself in future.

Another time, in a crowded pool, Clive saw a man fall awkwardly from the high diving board, hitting his arm on the way down and sinking. Searching underwater he found him drifting towards the drain and got him out of the water, resuscitating him and performing first aid on his arm until the ambulance arrived. Later the man came back to thank his rescuer, the bones of his arm held together with a steel plate.

Children were always most at risk when the place was seething with people. Clive once had to cross the width of the pool underneath the flailing legs of the masses to get to a young lad in trouble in mid-swimming lesson

– his instructor was fully-clothed on the poolside with a whistle, which she had used to alert the life guard. On another occasion he found a boy choking and panicking in the shallow end, closed his mouth with his hand and told him to blow through his nose – this cleared the obstruction in his airways. An impressed witness spoke to the manager about how he had handled the situation and Clive was commended for it.

The staff members themselves were not immune from peril in the water either. When several of them were indulging in horseplay one day, Clive was the only one who realised that the female lifeguard was neither enjoying it nor coping with it. The men around her were ducking her back under the water every time she surfaced and she was drowning. Clive rescued her and carried her to the first aid room where CPR proved unsuccessful, although he kept trying. Her life was eventually saved by the ambulance crew who managed to drain her lungs and start her breathing again on the way to the hospital.

This woman, though grateful, was not a conquest of Clive's but she was in the minority. With the return of his confidence and his impressive figure came the return of his promiscuity, and once again he drifted away from church because the life he was leading was incompatible with a close walk with Christ. This behaviour was very painful for Sheila who still loved him. Though the divorce was finalised, he saw his children regularly and, with his return to mental and physical health, she may have been entertaining hopes that they might get back together, but it was not to be.

Since the marriage ended, he had been living in a series of unsatisfactory rooms and flat-shares, waiting for the council to allocate him a flat of his own. The first one they offered him, little more than a cupboard, had been tastefully decorated by the previous occupant with a human skull complete with artistic red-paint 'bloodstains'! Fortunately he was accompanied on his visit to see it by an officer from the Ex-Serviceman's Mental Welfare Society, a charity that was helping and supporting him at this time. The officer went to the council and convinced them of the utter unsuitability of the place for a man with Clive's medical history, and he was offered instead a far better one, where he has lived ever since.

Fit and healthy, in his prime at thirty-two, usefully employed saving lives, and with a secure home, he still felt a nagging sense of something missing. Part of it was loss and bereavement for his army life and his family, but there was also something deeper that he had yet to identify. Despite his experiences with Christ, the concept of Him as the Be-All and End-All of life rather than just a desirable add-on was still foreign to him, and depression lurked waiting to pounce. Then, to the pool came a pretty, bubbly, friendly young girl called Carol and, for the second time in his life, Clive fell headlong in love.

*

She was half his age, cheerful and optimistic – completely his opposite in character, embodying everything he both craved and wanted to be. A solicitor's secretary, cheeky and provocative, she came from a family of liberal lifestyle and Clive was able to move her swiftly into his flat. Sex was still his main priority before companionship and friendship – but he felt that they were compatible in every respect.

Deborah, jealous for her mother, disliked Carol and predicted trouble, but Clive insists that in the five years they were together they never had a single row – an amazing thing, given that he was still drinking heavily. It never occurred to him that she might not consider this arrangement as permanent – that some day she might want children of her own and a man nearer her own age with less baggage. For him she was 'the one' and for the time being they were ecstatically happy.

With the encouragement of the British Legion and the Ex-Serviceman's Welfare Society (now Combat Stress) Clive applied for an army pension, a move which involved undergoing many medicals and tests and appearing before a tribunal to explain the symptoms and outcomes of his condition.

Accustomed to all things official never going his way, he was expecting to have his request denied, but to his amazement it was granted, and the pension was awarded. His interest in his job had palled since Carol had come along – now he could give it up. At last he could fulfil his long-held dream of visiting Israel. Better still, he could go there with Carol.

Israel was as wonderful as he had expected. The couple stayed first with friends of friends in Tel Aviv and travelled all over the country visiting just about every site of Biblical interest, including crossing the Negev Desert to the Red Sea, and looking at Jerusalem from the place where Jesus lamented over it (*Luke 13:34-35*). At the Church of the Nativity a Greek Orthodox priest took them up to the bell tower and claimed that, in his entire life, he had never told a lie. Then he took them down into the crypt beneath, showing them piles of tiny bones he said were 2000 years old, all boys of two or less, thought to be Herod's victims from the massacre of the innocents (*Matthew 2:16*). Carol was frightened and wanted to get out, but Clive felt nothing.

He remembers especially the site of Jesus' arrest at Gethsemane, the Garden Tomb and the place of the skull where the soldiers gambled for His clothes. It felt great to walk in His footsteps, but somehow not as overwhelming as he'd expected. There was a hard shell around Clive's heart that stopped this being a Spiritual experience, rather than just the holiday of a lifetime and the fulfilment of a long-held ambition. Everywhere they went he found himself searching compulsively, though he could not say what for.

The night he woke in the early hours on a pile of sand by the Jaffa Gate where he had fallen in a drunken stupor, he felt deeply ashamed. He remembered hearing how, in 1917, the victorious General Allenby had dismounted his horse and entered Jerusalem through this gate on foot out of respect, while Clive could only stagger through it and pass out. He even had to climb a drainpipe and break into their accommodation because the doors had been locked long ago.

Back home, life went on, as far as Clive was concerned, happily. He says now that Carol was 'Sheila's revenge' because here the roles were reversed and he was the one who loved more deeply while Carol was the one who remained always slightly detached, who never quite let him have all of her, whose focus was never one hundred percent on him. Even so he could not resist the temptation to stray, and had affairs with several other women. His gnawing feeling of unnamed loss and deprivation was always with him and he was no nearer to understanding it; he still drank, but there were no mental problems for another four years.

It was on another holiday, this one to Ibiza that they met Earhart and his girlfriend. Earhart seemed to gravitate to Clive and when they found out that
the German couple lived in Osnabrück, it seemed as though their meeting was both fortunate and fated. The four of them hung out together through the holiday and it ended with an invitation to Clive to come and stay with them and revisit old haunts. For someone who still pined for the happy security of the army, and who was forever searching for something to make him

complete, it was an irresistible offer, so it was agreed.

Carol did not go with him to Germany. It was his trip down memory lane, not hers, and it did not worry him particularly that she preferred to stay at home. He was looking forward to seeing his new friend and maybe looking up some old ones when he flew out there in the summer of 1983.

Almost as soon as he got there he felt that there was something wrong, though for a while he thought he must be imagining it. The couple's flat had a strange atmosphere to it; Earhart's brother was often present and his manner often appeared odd, even allowing for the language barrier. Earhart himself seemed subtly different from the way he had been in Spain. When Clive found unsavoury and unsettling drawings in the flat – Satan figured heavily in them – Earhart just laughed. He took to coming out with cryptic phrases like "We are doing a manipulation on you," which sounded vaguely threatening but meant nothing to Clive. The friendly, open man of Ibiza evaporated.

Then, out of the blue, Carol turned up. She had not come to join Clive or to share and rescue his unsatisfactory holiday – she had come to tell him that she was leaving him, that she could no longer live with his promiscuity and that she had found someone else. When she had told him face-to face and was sure he had taken it in and believed her, she went home again.

Clive remembers being utterly devastated, crying and crying, and then his memory becomes patchy. He had bought a china cat as a present for Earhart's girlfriend: he remembers holding it out to her on the palm of his hand, hearing a voice saying "the cat knows" and suddenly seeing the cat's mouth moving as if it was talking.

This classic delusion suggests that the emotional trauma was tipping him back over the edge into mental illness, but illness wasn't all he had to contend with here. He remembers Earhart, all trace of friendship gone, saying inexplicably, "If you were German you'd be dead by now." He remembers his feelings of utter terror and crying out to God to help him, and then seeming to hear an instruction to 'burn everything you have touched in the flat and leave'. He remembers hearing the Abba song, The Winner Takes it All and interpreting it as a taunt from the devil.

Out on the balcony he burnt everything he could remember touching and then left the flat. Walking the streets, freezing cold and shivering despite the warm weather, feeling as though he had a demon inside him that was clawing its way out through his chest, he knocked on a door at random and asked for a Bible. The young man who answered understood English and provided the Bible – he also called the police. As Clive stood looking at the open Bible and finding that he could not focus on any word of it, only on the spaces between the words, the officers came and took him to the police station, unsure how to handle him.

He did not have sufficient German to even begin to explain himself so he asked them for a Christian minister from one of the garrisons – any denomination – and got a padre accompanied by a military policeman. As coherently as he could manage he related to them what had happened to him, including Earhart's comments about manipulation and death. The RMP knew immediately what was going on – the names of Earhart and his brother and girlfriend were well known to the Military Police – and he told the padre that they were dealing with a circle of practising Satanists. Both men advised Clive that he should leave the country immediately, or he would very likely die.

He did not see either of them again. The German police released him and somehow he got to the airport by the method of repeating "flugplatz" (airport) at the train station until the staff put him on the right train. He has no idea how he coped with the turmoil and formalities of the airport or how he managed to get himself onto the right flight home. The plane seemed unusually rowdy, people were staring at him because he couldn't stop crying and he still felt freezing cold "as if something dead was around me." Convinced that he was possessed by at least one demon, he pushed his baggage trolley round and round Heathrow, with no idea what to do or where to go and every face around him appearing blank.

Eventually he organised himself enough to get a taxi home, paying the accommodating driver in deutschmarks because he had no English money on him. There was some relief at being back in the familiar and 'safe' surroundings of his own place, even if he was afraid of what he might have brought back there with him. Satanism in Osnabrück, especially in Army circles, must have been giving serious cause for concern at that time for the RMP to be so well-informed about it. Remembering his own activities there a decade before, it could be speculated that he was, in some way, reaping what he himself had sown.

If so it was a bitter harvest. Carol was still at the flat, having for the moment nowhere else to go, but in a relationship with another man. Clive's illness kicked in and he began to get delusions that he had supernatural powers and to try to make her do things like turning on a light by mind control. He stared at the sun again in defiance of God and felt as though it had burned through his eyes and out the back of his head – but he did not lose his sight as he so easily could have.

Finally, with Carol preparing to leave for good, a voice in his head told him to drink and he stood in the bathroom and drank water for six hours until it ran out of every pore and orifice. The next thing he remembers is waking up in Brookwood Mental Hospital with a pool of water under the bed. He had been sectioned. He had also drunk enough water to cause brain damage – but his brain was not damaged. God was protecting him still.

At the moment, though, the darkness of his illness overwhelmed him – he had now been diagnosed as having paranoid schizophrenia. Voices in his head told him to do strange and bizarre things and he obeyed them. He had constant paranoid fears of execution and murder – once in a washroom he felt as though he was being sexually assaulted by the devil – another time he remembers getting up off his bed and feeling himself knocked down by some invisible force, banging his head. He became convinced that he had the soul of Adolf Hitler.

Slowly he stabilised. One Sunday morning he woke to see a transparent figure at the end of his bed. It was an old man with flowing beard and hair, wearing a white robe and holding a long staff with a snake curled round it, head upwards. Before he could decide whether it was Moses with the brazen serpent (*Numbers 28:8-9*) or Asclepius, it vanished.

Sometime after this he was walking in the hospital grounds and saw a vision of a pile of jewelled crowns, one on top of the other, towering as high as he could see. A voice he knew to be the devil said. "I'll give you all these kingdoms if you worship me." It was an obvious parody of Christ's temptation in the wilderness (*Matthew 4:8-9*) and he believes if he had agreed then he would have been damned (*Hebrews 10:29-31*) but he met it with instinctive and emphatic rejection and walked on. With that choice a weight seemed to lift from him. He began to visit the church in the hospital grounds and, soon after, he was discharged.

The flat seemed unbearably empty without Carol. Clive would search out unlocked and unoccupied churches where he could sit and weep, giving vent to his uncontrollable broken-hearted sorrow. The loneliness was overwhelming. Even though he carried his Bible with him obsessively wherever he went, Clive felt that he needed a relationship, a woman in his life, to be whole and stable. He was still searching for what he lacked in all the wrong places – in this case a dating agency. He cannot claim that he wasn't warned, or shown what and Who he really needed. Alone in the living room of his flat he had a clear vision of the head and shoulders of Jesus wearing the crown of thorns – he sees it in his mind today as clearly as he saw it then. Not only does Jesus never take back His extended hand; He continues to hold it out when we ourselves let it go. Clive was deeply affected by the vision. But he still went ahead.

Janet was a divorcee with two daughters, and the whole affair was a disaster almost from the first. One of her daughters was tragically killed in a car accident, and then she became pregnant with Clive's child and promptly left him to go back to her husband. Clive had been fond of the lost daughter and was positive about the baby, seeing in it a link to life, a welcome responsibility and a reason to go on, but Janet, who had turned against him completely, told him he was to have no contact with it whatsoever, though he could send money. When the child, a boy, was born in Saudi Arabia where Janet's husband was working as a doctor, she would not allow Clive to send a card or present. In the event, the child died soon after birth and was buried out there. Janet did offer to send Clive pictures of the baby taken after death but he did not think he could handle that, so he said no.

Five

Captive in the Darkness

"You know that man who came in to be assessed for the dyslexia/dyspraxia therapy? Jackson, his name was..."

"I remember; tall bloke, well-built, softly spoken; seemed genuinely keen to improve himself. What about him?"

"He's a nutter."

"You what?"

"Manic Depression, paranoid schizophrenia, the lot."

"Oh no! And we were shut in the office here with him – anything could have happened! Someone should have warned us – well it shouldn't be allowed, should it? They should all be locked up. And we offered him a place, didn't we?"

"Only verbally, and who's going to take his word against ours? Massive bloke he was; we can say he scared us – well, we would have been scared if we'd known! No one's going to volunteer to work with him; I wouldn't put anyone in the position of asking them."

"I'm not sure we'll get away with that – there's laws against discrimination you know."

"Then we'll just keep stalling until he gives up and goes away..."

*

At this lowest of times, Clive's illness took a firm hold on him and much of the next two decades was taken up by cycles of psychotic episodes, alterations in his cocktail of medications, partial remissions and then relapses. At one time he took a train to Taunton and lived for two weeks on the streets before being admitted for a time to Tone Vale hospital, until he recovered enough to return home. Mental health professionals from the NHS and from Combat Stress did their best, but nothing seemed to work for long. Clive's memory at this time became fogged and, although he attempted to recount some of the traumatic experiences in his past to his therapists, his recall of timescale and order of events proved unreliable, and the accounts inconsistent. His explanations of the spiritual battle he felt he was enduring were largely written off as delusional and he was left to make what sense of it he could on his own.

Family difficulties, a common trigger of both bipolar and schizophrenia, played their part in Clive's fluctuating state of mind. Both of his children were afflicted with mental disorders, and his sense of responsibility for them and their problems frequently caused his own to flare up. Permission was sought, and granted, for all three sets of case notes to be sent to the Institute of Psychiatry to form part of a study into the role played by genetic factors in mental illness, but none of the three have ever had any feedback from this, or been informed of any conclusions the study may have come to.

Clive's relationship with his mother was never close after George died, though he kept up the connection. She had moved to a flat near Dartford and, in 1992, suffered a stroke that led to her being much incapacitated. Visiting her, Clive became friendly with one of her neighbours, a local small businessman who offered his help with Margaret since Clive lived so far away. The two men became friends and remained so even after Margaret had to be moved into a nursing home due to her worsening health.

In 1998, after six years of increasing disability, she died after falling from her bed and hitting her head – in exactly the same way as her own mother. Clive was with her in hospital at the end, saddened and much distressed at her refusal of Holy Communion. It brought home to him again that all he had been taught of Jesus had come from George – both verbally and by example. Still, she was the only real mother he had ever known, she had done her best for him and he loved and respected her and feared for her soul. To make things worse, his beloved Uncle Pat died at around the same time and it seemed as though everyone he relied upon was being taken from him at once.

After the funeral he found that a cousin who had visited from America during Margaret's last months had convinced her to alter her will – either because of Clive's illness or because of his adoptive status – and leave everything to her. Nothing could be done about it, but George, who had left all his worldly goods to his wife on the understanding that what was left would one day pass to his beloved son, would have been furious. It was a very low time, in Clive's life and he went through a deep valley of depression that took him some time to climb out of.

During his periods of good health Clive, supported by the mental health team that looked after him, made several attempts to work. Paid employment, had it been possible, would have greatly complicated his pension and benefits situation, but he did hold a voluntary position as an inspection diver until his imperfect eyesight and growing back pain prevented him from doing it safely.

As his physical health deteriorated and because of the longstanding nature of his psychiatric problems, finding work went from difficult to impossible. There was, and is still, much misunderstanding, fear and prejudice surrounding sufferers of psychiatric disorders, no doubt exacerbated by the lurid reporting in the press when any sort of related violence occurs. A tiny fraction of murders and assaults are committed by people with mental health issues – the vast majority come from those accounted 'sane' – but still the myth of the dangerous 'madman' persists.

A charity that claimed to specialise in improving the literacy and maximising the potential of dyslexics conducted a cordial and positive assessment interview with Clive and promised him help. Then they discovered he was schizophrenic and backpedalled, claiming that they had felt 'intimidated' by his size and felt unable to 'risk' their employees with him for fear of what he might do. A strongly-worded protest from the consultant psychiatrist led to them apologising, withdrawing their embargo provisionally and demanding a 'risk assessment'. At this point Clive decided he would feel so uncomfortable with them, knowing how they felt about him, that he was unlikely to get any benefit from their course, and he terminated the process.

Instead, he and his friend from Kent went into a business venture together, Clive investing much of the lump sum he had got from the army. The deal involved a new 'reverse engineering' technology that would scan artefacts and enable exact, collectible replicas to be made easily. A glance at the advert pages of any magazine shows how big a market this is, and the friend was convinced by it and investing his own money as well. It seemed like a good idea and a provision for the future.

That autumn the persistent worsening pain in his back was finally diagnosed as Ankylosing Spondylitis, a chronic, inflammatory arthritic disease of the lower spine. More pills were added to the many Clive already took, but only as palliatives – there is no cure for AS. Doctors are divided as to what causes it, but Clive attributes it to excessive running up and down cold, wet mountains with heavy army packs on his back. It was not cheering news and, over the next year, his mental health deteriorated once more to crisis-point and beyond. Combat Stress with their specialist understanding of the psychology of battle were of great benefit to him, as they had been for many years, but his interludes with them could only be temporary. Sooner or later he always had to come home.

He veered between believing he was Jesus trying to kill the devil, that he was the devil himself, or that the devil was trapped inside him. The multiple competing voices in his head made him feel like the man in the Bible possessed of a legion of demons. Christ had sent those demons into the swine and then the swine had been destroyed. (*Mark 5:1-13*) It made perfect sense to Clive that if the devil was inside him and he wanted to kill the devil he must kill himself.

With a pair of scissors in the bath he cut his left arm as deeply as he could. But then, he says, “Something bigger and stronger than me gave me a fantastic desire to live.” Sometime later he was picked up in the street by the police, naked and bleeding heavily, and taken to A&E, from where he was swiftly transferred to the psychiatric unit. Catatonic on arrival, the following day he had no idea how he had got there and great difficulty in believing that he had arrived with no clothes on. Terrified that closing the cut would 'seal in' the devil, he refused to have it stitched and did not like the nursing staff even touching it. During the two months he was there, it slowly healed by itself.

He did not tell anyone that he believed he was hosting the devil and remembers being afraid of another patient who described in group therapy sessions how he wanted to 'behead the devil', fearing this man would recognise him as the target. He had constant feelings of paranoia, convinced that he would be murdered if he stayed in the unit. After a while and against the doctors' advice he discharged himself, went home and clawed his way back to a semblance of rationality.

But not for long. Within two months the conviction that the devil was inside him and could be destroyed by his death returned stronger than ever. Endlessly badgered from within, he ripped the cable from his computer and headed for the woods, apologising out loud to the apostle Paul, who had lived with his own 'messenger of Satan' (*2Corinthians 12:7-9*) and to his friend Peter who had tried to help him. He managed to climb a tree, tie one end of the cable to a branch and the other round his neck and jump. The cable broke and he hit the ground heavily.

He got up, returned home, collected two neckties which he knotted together and tied round his neck, went up to the second floor of the flats, attached the loose end of the ties to a post and jumped off the balcony. The ties also broke and he hit the ground again and this time injured his weak back. Crawling into his own flat he managed to get onto his bed and determined to lay there until he starved, but a voice told him, “You don’t know how long that will take.” So he called an ambulance instead and two paramedics he describes as “absolute heroes” strapped him to a back board and took him to hospital.

His back was not broken and he soon found himself in the familiar surroundings of the psychiatric unit under twenty-four hour surveillance. The thought came to him that maybe he was not ‘meant’ to die by his own hand. After all, logic told him, if he waited long enough, one day he would inevitably die anyway.

With the relinquishing of his death wish, there in the psychiatric unit Clive underwent what he believes was a life or death struggle with his illness and with the devil, who was attacking him through it. He ate very little, and that mainly vegetables since they went swiftly through the system, believing Jesus' words about food in Matthew 15:17 to mean that demons could enter his body with his food. Once it was as though he could see inside his own body with all its workings, lit up like a museum display, and remembers vomiting up "a clear silver liquid."

Haunted by memories of the artworks of Hieronymus Bosch, he had long arguments with the devil in his head, sometimes experiencing him as a giant serpent writhing violently inside his skull until he understood why some people take a gun and blow their own brains out. Voices whispered to him with seductive suggestions about witchcraft and necromancy like that practised by Saul's Witch of Endor (*1Samuel 28:7-16*).

Somehow he found the strength to resist. Whoever he was persuaded to believe himself to be, however loathsome he felt himself and his actions, he knew beyond any doubt that God is good and that he loved Him, and nothing the devil put him through could either surpass that or change it. With the remains of his sanity and strength, with grim, bloody-minded determination, with absolutely no encouragement from a sceptical and atheistic staff, he clung on to Jesus Christ.

His tenacity was rewarded. The doctors found the right balance of drugs, and he found the right balance of mind for him to return once more, battle-scarred and weary, to his own home.

Voices still talked to him as though he was Jesus but now he knew beyond all doubt that he was not, and that they were lying and trying to deceive him. Jesus Christ is utterly without sin; Clive Jackson was a sinner. Jesus Christ says "It is finished" (*John 19:30*) and that He has won the battle and the devil is defeated (*Colossians 2:15*). Clive had been listening to the devil's lies and trying to do it all over again.

He knew couldn't go on this way alone. He needed support from people who understood that the devil is real. He needed other Christians.

He needed the church.

Six

Survival Rations

"'In the last days it will be,' God declares, 'that I will pour out My Spirit on all flesh, and your sons and your daughters shall prophesy, and your young men shall see visions and your old men shall dream dreams. Even upon My slaves, both men and women, in those days I will pour out My Spirit.'"
(Acts 2:17-18)

*

Clive is reasonably sure now that the figure he saw at the end of his Brookwood Hospital bed was Moses, who lifted the brazen serpent in the wilderness at God's command to heal the Israelites (*Numbers 21: 8-9*) – an event

Jesus referred to when He predicted the manner of His own death and explained how it would bring life to all who believed in Him (*John 3:14-15*). That vision, heralding the beginning of a slow and stuttering progress back to comparative health, was the first of many increasingly detailed waking-state dreams that Clive experienced. Some related personally to him, some were of actual Biblical events, some were Biblical in nature but of events not related in the Bible.

Both doctors and Christian friends of Clive have been sceptical of the validity of these episodes, inclined to attribute them to his illness. Indeed he has at times been subject to the hallucinations common to sufferers of bipolar disorder and schizophrenia but, in the peace of his current mental stability, he is convinced that he can tell the difference between these incidents and the genuine visions.

Traditional denominations tend to shy away from such happenings and relegate them to times long past, but the Bible clearly states that dreams and visions will occur in 'the last days' and it documents many instances of God communicating in this way, in both Old and New Testaments. In an age when most ordinary people did not read and write at all, a picture was worth much more than a thousand words. Evangelical churches today tend to be far more open to the possibility of the Spirit providing 'pictures' to the open-minded believer.

Clive remembers all of his visions with great clarity, but he cannot accurately say what order they came in or when exactly many of them occurred. He does not understand all of them – why for instance was he given an unpleasantly close view of the sickening 'entertainment' of the Roman area? – but their upshot may become clearer to him as time goes on. He did not, at the time, understand the sight of Christ, in a pose similar to Rio's giant Redeemer statue, standing on the streets of Waterloo and being totally ignored by every passerby, but he does now. All these visions were very real and immediate to him, feeling like an experience he participated in with all his senses rather than an observed event, like a film or play. I relate them here just as he told them to me.

Finding himself aboard a US battleship he heard the tannoy announcement "Now hear this!" repeated several times and was among the sailors below deck as they responded in haste and with apprehension, rushing to get topsides. Clive searched among them, looking at every face, knowing he was looking for his biological father, sensing he was somewhere close in the throng, but not finding him. On another occasion he found himself on a deep dive, swimming along the starboard side of the same ship, sunk to the sea bed, and knowing it was his father's grave.

He saw an Air Sea Rescue helicopter over a stretch of water he knew to be the English Channel, a man looking out of the side of it, searching for Clive. Many years ago there was a rumour that a woman he had an affair with at an outward bound centre might have been pregnant, but he never saw her again or heard any more of her. He now suspects that there was a child, that it may have grown up to be the ASR man and may possibly have tried to track him down at some time. If so, he didn't succeed.

Another time he was in a vertical shaft, not falling but being drawn inexorably downwards. Below him at the bottom he could see the figure of an idol holding in its arms a vast flaming crucible. As he got nearer and nearer the heat became worse and worse and he knew there was no way back and that he was headed for the crucible of fire and would be there forever. Then, coming out of his own mouth he heard the words, "Love can't burn in those flames," and instantly he was free and the vision was gone. He sees this as a fairly obvious case of the devil trying to make him think he was bound for hell when, in truth, he has the God Who is Love within him (*Ephesians 3:17*) and is therefore eternally safe.

That wasn't his only vision of hell. Another time he saw it as a vast empty place of scorching sand with vast circles in it. He seemed to be told that this was the "birthplace of Satan" but he knows that Satan was created by God and was originally an angel, cast out of heaven and flung to earth after his rebellion (*Luke 10:18*). Maybe this was where he landed and began his earthly satanic career? In a cave, a terrifying gnarled and dreadlocked ancient man sat staring at Clive across a huge flat stone. Not Satan but, even more frightening, a representation of what Clive might become. He remembers vividly the feelings of crushing dread and overpowering terror. There was no doubt that this was the worst place anyone could be.

In contrast he has also been shown a preview of heaven, with a multitude of people dressed in white, a place so wonderful he knew he wanted to be there forever and was bitterly disappointed when he found himself returned to normality. At first it troubled him that he saw only men and doesn't remember any women there, but Jesus tells us there will be no marriage in heaven and all of us will be like the angels (*Matthew 22:29-30*) and Paul says in one of his letters that hierarchies of race, class and gender no longer apply to Christians but all are one in Christ Jesus (*Galatians 3:27-29*). Clive's subconscious translated the unimaginably glorious resurrection bodies of heaven (*Philippians 3:20-21*) into something his earthly mind could process. A woman having a similar vision would most likely have seen only women.

In an elaborate scene reminiscent of various allegories, he saw a low, small-wheeled cart drawn by six white oxen with golden horns and followed by six more. On the cart was a cage and sitting in the cage, chained, was a Man Clive knew to be Jesus despite the fact that He was clean shaven and His hair was in long braids, Greek fashion. Clive remembers circling the cage and looking at Him from all sides as He sat, calm and serene, His arms resting on His knees. He remembers clinging to the side of the cart, face to face with Him, asking "Who am I?" and then dropping to the ground by the wheel of the cart in time to see it running over a small boulder and crushing it. The cart stopped by a very large building, not civic or military but residential; Clive describes it as like an anthill with many windows. Jesus stood up, His chains fell from Him and dropped to the floor, and then the vision slowly faded.

So, if it was allegorical, what did it all mean? At the time, Clive was afraid the crushed boulder represented him, but Christ's chains falling off surely meant that the malign authority behind the tumbrel had been overcome by Him. Clive's question to Christ is reminiscent of his childhood haunting of churches asking Who and where Jesus was; by the time of the vision he knew the answer to that – now he was far more worried by the question of who he was himself. The falling off of Christ's chains was probably symbolic of Clive's own freedom in Him. In the words of Charles Wesley, "My chains fell off, my heart was free; I rose, went forth and followed Thee." (*Luke 4:18, Acts 12:7, Acts 16:26*)

In a true occurrence of the Old Testament (*1Samuel 21:1-6*), he saw David and his followers in the temple with the priest, Ahimelech, who gave them the bread of the Presence to eat. David was to the right of the altar and his men to the left. This incident was, of course, quoted by Jesus when the Pharisees charged His disciples with 'harvesting' on the Sabbath – they had merely stripped a few grains of corn to eat as they passed through the field (*Matthew 12:1-8, Mark 2:23-28, Luke 6: 1-5*). The Sabbath was meant to be a blessing to man, not man a slave to the Sabbath – David did not scruple to eat the holy bread, and he was 'a man after God's own heart' (*1Samuel 13:14*). God is not looking for slavish adherence to religious laws – for more Pharisees – He has too many of those as it is. A comforting reminder for someone like Clive, who has led a far from conventional Christian life.

Another vision of the Temple was from many centuries later, when he saw a priest he believes to be Caiaphas talking to Jesus. It was the occasion when Jesus said "Destroy this Temple and in three days I will build it up" and the priest replied "This Temple has been under construction for forty-six years and you will raise it up in three days?" not realising He meant His body (*John 2:19-21*).

Clive clearly saw the priest, dressed in white standing in an alcove in the wall, which is puzzling until one looks the conversation up in the Bible and finds it was immediately preceded by Jesus, consumed by zeal for His Father's house, overturning tables and clearing the Temple of moneychangers with a whip. The priest tucking himself out of the way suddenly makes perfect sense!

Again a jump forward in time to the days of the early church, and a violent scene of a man Clive knew to be James, the brother of Jesus and leader of the Jerusalem Christians, being thrown over a parapet near the top of a high building – maybe the Temple again. He also saw other companions of Jesus there. This incident is not mentioned in the Bible and at first seemed unlikely, as Josephus, the contemporary Jewish historian, says James was stoned to death. The custom in those days was for the victim to be taken outside the city and thrown from a high cliff before being stoned (as in *Luke 4:29*), not from any sort of building.

But Eusebius, a later church father and respected historian himself, gives a fuller picture. James was asked by the Pharisees to address the Passover crowds and convince them that Jesus was merely a gifted rabbi and not the Christ. This was most likely to have happened at the Temple and it is quite probable that other followers of Jesus were present. In the event he did precisely the opposite, testifying that his brother was in truth the Son of God. To shut him up and frighten his audience the Pharisees threw him down, but the fall did not kill him and then they stoned him. Eventually he died when a staff was thrown at his head. This very public martyrdom only served to increase the number of believers in Jesus.

At a time when Clive was living alone at his flat and depressed about his life and lack of a job he witnessed the wonderful vision of a waterfall of stars pouring down at him out of the night sky "as if they were being poured out of a jug" – glowing white spheres "like Christmas lights" that followed him indoors before fading. He was astounded and elated to find in his Bible that *"every perfect gift is from above, coming down from the Father of lights, which whom there is no variation or shadow due to change." (James 1:17)* And indeed his heavenly Father has never failed to provide for his needs, whatever his situation and capabilities.

Clive knows exactly where he was when he had the vision of Paul in prison. He was in the psychiatric unit, just prior to his last great struggle there with the devil. Paul was a short, stocky, olive-skinned man, sitting in a cave-like cell with a metal grille door, through which could be seen a Roman soldier on guard. Seated in the middle of the cell and dressed in a leather tunic, the apostle was writing busily and did not look up or speak. Clive somehow knew that the passage he was writing was the one in his letter to the Ephesians about putting on the full armour of God (*Ephesians 6:11-17*). *"For our struggle is not against enemies of blood and flesh, but against the rulers, against the authorities, against the cosmic powers of this present darkness, against the spiritual forces of evil in the heavenly places."* Seldom has advice and instruction proved so necessary and so timely.

On a later occasion, sitting in the unit's dining room, he saw a massive bunch of plum-sized grapes, similar to those found by the Hebrew spies when they went into Canaan to find out what it was like (*Numbers 13:23*). He must have been close by then to the 'Promised Land' of a sound mind (*Luke 8:35*) but, like the Israelites, he would still need courage and belief to take possession of it – and to keep hold of it once he had it.

Seven

Peacekeeping

"Excuse me, I know this is going to sound odd, but I was praying and Jesus told me to feed His sheep but not to go alone. Once I had a vision, you see, of Jesus standing with His arms held out and people just walking past Him like lost sheep, ignoring Him – I think it was somewhere near Waterloo. Anyway, I'm sure 'Feed My sheep' means the homeless and I'm told the two of you go up to London once a week to take food and things and minister to the homeless. Can I come with you?"

"Of course; we'd be glad to have you. We're going tonight, actually – do you want to come tonight?"

"Yes please. Whereabouts is it you go?"

"Waterloo – but surely you knew that?"

"No."

*

In Clive's local town of Knaphill there is a cafe run by the local churches and staffed mainly by volunteers. It's called the King's House Coffee Shop and, like the King Himself, is warmly welcoming to all. In the summer of 2005, Clive was sitting at a table when he was approached by two men – one he knew, a friend called John, the other a stranger in a brown mac, who was introduced to him as Peter Thompson.

Clive and Peter hit it off at once and were to have many long talks that helped enormously both to inform Clive's faith and dispel many of his worries and doubts. He had recently began attending his parish church of Holy Trinity, with the idea of taking the devil he was still half sure resided within him, into the presence of God. Unpleasant images had pursued him even there, the feeling of a veil across his face, of his head being pushed down a foul toilet. It was a blessed relief to him to have a friend he could discuss Spiritual matters with at length, someone who would listen and not condemn, though he was naturally cautious about what he revealed at first.

Peter – the Reverend Doctor Peter Thompson – was a retired canon and a former surgeon who had run hospitals in Burma with his wife before they, like all foreigners, had been obliged to leave by the military Junta. A friend of the revered theologian, John Stott, and vastly experienced, he found a lot of what Clive had to tell him difficult and astonishing.

Later that year in a Christian bookshop in Woking Clive found a book by David Devenish called *'Demolishing Strongholds: Effective Strategies for Spiritual Warfare'* Reading it, he found that his experiences weren't peculiar only to him, that the devil attacked others in similar fashion, and that there were ways of dealing with it. Both the book and Peter Thompson, along with the ministry of Holy Trinity, taught him a lot about discipleship. At last he began to understand fully what it means to follow Jesus Christ, and to read and meditate on Scripture.

Knowing what was required did not make it easy to perform. His illnesses still dogged him and there were still difficulties, lapses, misunderstandings and hurts. He was forced to give up his voluntary work as an instructor and lifeguard for Woking Dolphins Swimming Club – a job he loved – because of his bad back, and then the business venture he had gone into with his friend collapsed leaving them both vastly out of pocket. But there was also a new, closer relationship with Jesus and a new confidence that Clive belonged to Him, and this somehow lifted him and kept him from the total collapse that might have resulted from these knock-backs before.

In the spring of 2008 the doctors were inspired to put him onto a new drug that could have a slow but profound effect. It would not cure his symptoms totally, they told him, but, if it worked, it should go a long way towards weakening his darker thoughts. It worked, and what it did, in effect, was give him control over what he thought about – a luxury he had not experienced in very many years.

This was a major breakthrough. For the first time since Towyn beach, Clive's mind was clear of the constant clamour of voices accusing, condemning, taunting, instructing, confusing and breaking him down. He was left feeling almost bereft. Strangely the loss of the voices seemed to underline the loneliness of many of his days. So much of his time had been taken up with the constant struggle inside his head – what was he to do with that time now? The silence was deafening but, as always, the Lord was in the silence (*1Kings 19:11-13*).

*

For several years now, the instrument of Christ's grace and support to Clive has been his local church, Holy Trinity Knaphill. Their acceptance of him and his sometimes bizarre words and behaviour, their love and their prayers have formed a large part of his current stability and peace. Under the influence of the gospel and God's people the Holy Spirit has been free to work and, gradually, over a period of time, the drinking, the womanising and the compulsive lying have stopped.

It is a deep sadness to him that both his children seem to have inherited his predisposition to mental illness and he has often been plagued with feelings of guilt over this – once to the point of a drug overdose. He still has to resist temptation, he is still subject to spiritual attack, on one occasion objects have been flung, poltergeist-fashion, around his flat, but he has set his sights resolutely on Jesus and kept them there.

"God knows that a part of my brain doesn't work properly," he says. "But He is *'our refuge and strength, an ever-present help in trouble'* and Jesus said *'Come to Me all you who are weary and burdened and I will give you rest.'"* (*Psalm 46:1 and Matthew 11:28*) He has clung to these truths when his own mind has betrayed him, when Christian brothers and sisters have lacked sympathy or misunderstood his condition, when doctors have dismissed his faith as just another delusion. The devil knows he can harass bipolar and schizophrenia sufferers with impunity because nothing they say about him will be believed, even sometimes by people who really should know better (*2Corinthians 2:11*).

If he indulges it, there is still within him a fear that he might slip back, but he looks to another favourite scripture *"perfect love casts out fear"* and believes if he always puts love first he leaves no room for the devil. Spending time with him as his biographer, I have seen this in action with his neighbours, friends, and customers at the King's House Coffee Shop, and it is a humbling and convicting experience.

Once, while praying in church, the scripture *"Feed my sheep,"* came to his mind, closely followed by "But don't go alone." (*John 21:17*) He had the idea that this instruction had to do with feeding the homeless, so he consulted a lay reader about it. Unknown to him, two men from the church went regularly with food and supplies for the homeless to Waterloo Bridge, just where he had seen the vision of the ignored Christ, His arms open in invitation. He joined them that night and has been part of their weekly ministry there ever since.

God can and does turn everything into an opportunity to learn and for faith to grow. In the summer of 2010 Clive was recovering from an infection but determined not to let it prevent him from going on holiday. He was due to spend some time in Wales where Jane, the wife of a military friend works as a carer for three men with mental illnesses and where he is welcomed every Christmas as one of the family. After five days there they were to travel on to Orkney for a further week. The neighbour who helped Clive to the taxi for the station noticed he was unsteady on his feet, but despite this he arrived safely.

It wasn't until they were on the coach from Denbigh to the Orkneys that Clive's health really began to deteriorate. He began to shake uncontrollably, as if with a fever and this turned into fits. Jane and the coach driver decided the best thing was to take him to Raigmore Hospital in Inverness, which was the nearest, and check him in at A&E. Admitted and on life support, his seizures increased in number and duration until he was convinced he would die, and the medical staff performed more and more scans and tests on him. He remembers that he was conscious of being unconscious, in thick darkness between life and death. Eventually he was given anti-epilepsy drugs, which stopped the fits.

He was sustained during all of this by the prayers of Jane and by phone calls from her and also from Sheila. Remembering the Bible story of Jesus curing an epileptic and then telling the baffled disciples, “This sort only comes out by prayer,” (*Mark 9:17-29*) he feels Jane’s prayers for him played a major part in his recovery. The Spanish lady specialist who treated Clive refused to believe there was any Spiritual aspect because she saw the symptoms stop when she administered the drugs. She did not think to question Who made the component parts of the drugs and gave men the inspiration to invent and manufacture them, or Who gifted her with her skills and knowledge and placed her where she was. As the Bible tells us, “The earth is the Lord’s and all that is in it; the world and those who live in it.” (*Psalm 24:1*) “All things came into being through Him, and without Him not one thing came into being.” (*John 1:3*).

At this time Clive had what he calls a ‘terrifying internal fit of the mind.’ For some years a constant theme of his thoughts had been frustration at his inability to earn money and improve his lot; even though warned by Peter Thomson about the impossibility of ‘serving two masters’, get-rich-quick schemes had an irresistible pull on his mind and imagination. Not long before his holiday he had seen an article, he believes it was in the Telegraph, telling how, cleverly bought, restored and sold, chairs could be more lucrative that property. He had been angry at the lack of capital, knowledge and opportunity that barred him from things like this.

Now he found himself in a richly appointed room containing a semi-circle of sumptuously decorated chairs. They were fabulously beautiful but, looking closely at them, he saw that they had no life or love in them – they were dead things, just furniture. He felt as though he was being given a choice – offered what he'd thought he wanted in return for his soul. He felt the danger, rejected the idea, and the tempting image left him.

Another long-term resentment was the fact that his invisible disability attracted far less sympathy and understanding than any physical disability would – he had become accustomed to thinking of the physically disabled as 'better off' than him. All around him in the Raigmore ward were many examples of the wrongness of this thinking. He found himself unable to walk and had to 'learn' to do so again, for no medical reason that anyone could ascertain. Another lesson that we should all be content with the hand God has dealt us? Clive now walks as well as he ever did. We may reap what we sew but Christ's grace is stronger, deeper, and more bountiful than anything else in creation.

Two weeks later he was discharged and facing a mammoth journey back to Surrey by taxis paid for through his travel insurance. As he got into the first one that was to take him from Inverness to Edinburgh, he saw a magnificent rainbow and remarked to the driver that it was a sign from God. It turned out that the driver was a Christian too and they talked Spiritual matters all the way to the Scottish capital, Clive feeling strong and secure and that God's hand was on him. In Edinburgh he was handed over to the second driver for the longer leg of his journey and found that this one was a young Muslim man. Amazingly the changeover was blessed by yet another rainbow and, encouraged by this, he engaged the man in talk about God and they too talked freely about their faiths and God's goodness all the way home. Further recovery time was needed from his physical ailments, but he knew he was 'better' in all the ways that mattered.

He never had epilepsy before and does not have it now. *"...keep alert; like a roaring lion your adversary the devil prowls around looking for someone to devour. Resist him, steadfast in your faith..." (1Peter 5:8-9)*

*

Clive's purpose in writing this book is not only to tell the whole truth and leave nothing hidden, but to warn people that they have a soul, that eternity is a very long time and they have a choice of where they will spend it, and that no one can sink so low that God cannot reach them. He is a walking affirmation that, once we claim it, nothing – not even our own actions – can separate any of us from the love of Christ (*Romans 8:33-39*).

"If I make my bed in hell, You are there," says Psalm 139. *"If I say, 'surely the darkness shall cover me, and the light around me become night,' even the darkness is not dark to You; the night is as bright as the day, for darkness is as light to You."*

There has been much darkness in Clive's life, and at times he has almost been overwhelmed by it – almost but never completely, because he has never been deserted by his Saviour. The enemy of all mankind has attacked him at every turn but, thanks to the Lord's protection, he has been: *"afflicted in every way but not crushed; perplexed but not driven to despair; persecuted but not forsaken; struck down but not destroyed. Always carrying the death of Jesus... so that the life of Jesus may also be made visible."* (*2Corinthians 4:8-10*). It is his dearest wish that reading how he has been brought through his trials will open others up to the truth about ourselves and the world we live in.

The Bible tells us that, *"our struggle is not against flesh and blood, but against the rulers, against the authorities, against the powers of this dark world and against the spiritual forces of evil in the heavenly realms."* And therefore we should *"take up the full armour of God, so that when the day of evil comes you may be able to stand your ground and having done everything, to stand firm."* (*Ephesians 6:12-13*)

We can only take up God's full armour if we know Him and follow Him. The Lord has been a constant unwavering light to Clive in the darkness, this same Light is there for all men and women, no matter where they've been and what they've done (even if they've been nowhere and done nothing) and it's freely available just for the asking.

Epilogue

Some of you may have picked up this book out of an interest in mental illness, in true-life stories, because you know me, or because you've met Clive and wanted to find out what made him the man he is today. If you have no Christian experience of your own, you may be wondering exactly what the deal is with God.

Well, the deal with God is His son, Jesus Christ, because the only way to God – the only way to experience the wonderful heaven and avoid the terrible hell mentioned in this book – is through knowing, trusting and believing in Jesus Christ.

In these days of political correctness it's frowned upon to say, "There is one definitive truth and this is it." Strangely enough this squeamishness only seems to apply to frightening, life-defining issues of God and eternity – when it comes to science or accountancy, for instance, people are only too keen for there to be one incontrovertible answer.

The real truth encompasses all areas. The God Who made the universe, Who created the earth along with everything and everyone on it, Who invented science and accountancy as well as beauty and wonder, has made His Son the pivotal point upon which the soul of every human being is balanced.

He created us to be holy and perfect like Him, but we chose to fall in with the devil's suggestions for sin because they sounded far more like fun and freedom than staying close to God did. We may not hear a literal voice in our heads, but it speaks to every one of us and we all listen and go along with it to a greater or lesser extent. How far we proceed in our wrong-doing is irrelevant: we have all sinned and fallen short of the glory of God.

God cannot abide sin and no sinful person can go to heaven. We all know where sinners end up and, left to ourselves, that's where we're heading.

But God loves us, and He wants to save us all from the consequences of our own actions, so Jesus – wholly God and wholly man – came here to us. He did so entirely voluntarily, in full knowledge of what He faced, and He lived the perfect sinless life we were designed to live – the life we need to live to have any sort of communion with God.

Then He died, horribly, and as He died he took the sins of all of us – past, present and future – onto His own shoulders and then He took the full force of God's wrath for every single one of them. Any suffering we might go through pales into insignificance beside that.

Three days later He rose from the dead, having paid the price to buy us back from

Satan, and now, again, we have a choice – a second chance to do the right thing. Accept His offer, let go of our sins, take the hand of Jesus, follow Him, and spent eternity in heaven with Him. Or reject what He did, spurn His offer of free-to-us redemption, remain in the service of the devil. Experience God's awful wrath for ourselves. End up in hell.

You might not think you're serving the devil but, let me tell you, my friend, there are only two sides in this battle and there is no neutral territory. Either you're with Jesus Christ, or you're with the devil. And there are only two ultimate destinations, heaven or hell.

The choice is yours.

The one thing you won't be able to say is "But nobody told me..."

Combat Stress

Combat Stress – formerly the Ex-Servicemen's Welfare Society – is the UK's leading military charity specialising in the care of veterans' mental health, and their services are free of charge to the veteran.

Since 2005 the number of ex-service men and women seeking their help has risen by 72%, and they have a current caseload of more than 4,300 individuals (May 2010). This already includes 102 veterans who have served in Afghanistan and 400 who served in Iraq.

In March 2010 their patron, HRH the Prince of Wales, launched a major fundraising campaign – The Enemy Within Appeal.

This £30 million, three-year appeal is designed to help treat the escalating number of psychologically injured veterans who are turning to Combat Stress for help, by:

- Establishing 14 Community Outreach Teams nationwide

- Enhancing clinical treatment at their three short-stay treatment centres

Visit their website at

www.combatstress.org.uk

for more information or to make a donation.

Donations can also be sent to:

The Chief Executive,
Combat Stress,
Tyrwhitt House,
Oaklawn Road,
Leatherhead,
Surrey
KT22 0BX

ND - #0251 - 080726 - C0 - 197/132/13 - PB - 9781780353463 - Gloss Lamination